When you feel like screaming

Practical Help for Frustrated Moms

SUE HEIMER

ISBN-13: 978-1986679176
ISBN-10: 1986679179

DEDICATION

This book is dedicated to my four sons, Seth, Levi, Casey and Brock. It is a privilege to be your "perfect" imperfect mom.

And to my husband Curt - After 34 years you still call me "my girl." It is an honor to be your wife.

CONTENTS

INTRODUCTION

This book has developed over ten years. Yes, ten. The first drafts looked very different than the book you are now holding. Earlier outlines held pages of statistics as I shared the data collected on the "why" we moms lose it and yell at our kids. After sending sample chapters to my friends to read and give feedback, the comments I received back showed a pattern. *"Please share fewer survey results and data. I know I scream and need encouragement, ideas and strategies for change".* I also heard the echo of *"I am a very busy mom. Omit the fluff and keep it short and to the point."* I listened and did; on both accounts.

I would love to say, *"Brew a cup of coffee, curl up on the couch and enjoy this book."* Yeah, like in our dreams. For most of us, that is not going to happen. The chapters are purposely short (most are two pages). Most likely mom, you will put this book on your nightstand and read a few pages a night. Or it will be in the bottom of your purse and a chapter will be read while waiting in the carpool line or soccer practice.

Wherever and whenever you read this book, as you turn the pages, may you feel validated, understood, encouraged and empowered with practical tools for change.

I cannot guarantee you will be a "screamless" mom when you finish reading this book and put the tips into practice. However, I believe you will "scream less" today than you did yesterday. It is an honor to journey with you.

CHAPTER 1
I Didn't Start out Screaming!

"When I lose it with my kids, I immediately feel guilt and shame."
Stacy from Switzerland

"When I lose it, or yell, I feel I have hurt my kid's feelings. I recall how I felt when my mom yelled at me, I feel I've become her."
Sheyla from Holland

There is a sign, posted on a rural, rutted, dirt road in Canada, which reads, "Be careful which rut you choose, for you will be in it the next 35 miles." Screaming is a rut, a poor form of communication that once you choose it, can be difficult to escape.

The New Webster's Dictionary gives the following definition of screaming: to cry out with a loud, shrill voice. The definition alone echoes in my ears, like nails on a chalkboard. Webster's also describes a rut as a habitual pattern of behavior.
Intrigued by these definitions, I built up the courage and looked up the word *habit*. This explanation did not add comfort to my research. It read: habit; a disposition, to act

constantly in a certain manner, usually acquired by frequent repetition.

Ouch — all of this is sounding way too familiar. By looking up these few words, we can assume that screaming is a habit. The exciting news, among this painful revelation, is that habits can be broken!

The habit of screaming reminds me of my old refrigerator. When the compressor kept running and the ice cream was soft, we knew it was time to replace it. Needing to save for a new one, (Nope, I don't have $1200.00 lying around that says, "For your new fridge...") we decided to bring the spare up from the basement to begin the process of switching out the fridges on a Sunday night. By the time our sons dragged and pulled the replacement up the basement steps (my son told me it was like dragging a baby elephant) and I had switched all the food over, our nerves were frazzled and our patience shot. From past lessons of disastrous results, I knew better than to suggest they move the old fridge out of the middle of the kitchen and out to the garage for disposal. We all agreed to wait until Monday night when we all were rested and ready for the final leg of the fridge's journey.

Monday morning, it soon became evident that the old fridge in its new location (in the middle of my kitchen) was not convenient. It seemed every step I took had to be re-thought as I worked around the obstacle. It was annoying, unproductive, and aggravating. However, Monday evening proved to be too busy to get a quorum of family members together to move out the fridge....and there it sat. It remained parked in my kitchen all day Tuesday. By

Wednesday, I hardly noticed the fridge anymore; walking around it had become such a habit.

On Wednesday afternoon, my friend Sid came to visit. "Sue," she said, as she entered the kitchen. "Why do you have a refrigerator in the middle of your kitchen?" To Sid, who had not grown accustomed to the giant object, it looked ridiculously out of place.

"Yeah, I don't know why it is STILL here. At first it was such a hindrance, but now that I am used to it, I hardly even notice it," I explained.

And it is like that with screaming. At first it surprises us, maybe embarrasses us, but then as time goes on, we hardly even recognize it anymore for what it is; a destructive, poor form of communication.

Questions

1. Have you considered yelling a habit, a reaction, or something else?
2. If yelling is indeed a habit, do you think you can break this habit?

$Screaming$
is a habit.

The exciting news is that
HABITS CAN
BE BROKEN!

CHAPTER 2
Comraderie, Hope, and Change

Several months ago, while speaking at a conference, I was going through my morning routine in the bathroom. Somewhat groggy from the previous late night, I put on my deodorant and started to brush my teeth. As I was brushing away, my armpits started to feel warm. They got warmer, and then hot! "What is going on?" I thought to myself as I grabbed my deodorant can. Upon inspection, I realized I had applied roll-on "Icy Hot" instead of deodorant! Did I mention the words, "Eucalyptus Scent?" No amount of rubbing with a wet cloth would take away the burn and I had no time to shower again, as I was due at the conference in a few minutes. So, with the pits on fire, I drove with my arms up in the air like a chicken, trying to air them out. The results of the mishap stayed with me all day and I had a faint smell of eucalyptus surrounding me wherever I went. Let's just say I felt no muscle aches in those armpits all day!

This experience reminds me of the habit of screaming. Mothers use this form of communication, because we think it will produce results. Grabbing onto it, without looking closely at what the outcome may be, we use it liberally, only to find the effect not quite what we had envisioned. The residue leaves a wounded heart and crushed spirit in a child and, for us, a fair amount of internal guilt.

A scene transpired on a spring day that will forever be etched in my mind. It was one of those ah-ha moments in mothering that one does not forget. I had sent our third son, five-year-old Casey, out to play in the yard. I was preoccupied with trying to get his baby brother Brock down for a nap. I was exhausted from a sleepless night in which Brock had been awake multiple times because of a fever. When Casey was born, I thought he would be my last, so I had lovingly called him my "Littlest Angel" since birth, a term of endearment which stuck even though he was not my youngest anymore. After rocking the baby to sleep, I tiptoed out of his room and gingerly closed the door. Finally, I could have some respite and maybe a quick nap! Just then my Casey came bounding into the room.

"Mommy, Mommy, look what I found!" he exclaimed.
The noise had awoken his baby brother and Brock began to wail. I was so frustrated, I shouted, "Now look what you've done!" and hurried back into the bedroom to rock the baby back to sleep. A little while later, after coaxing the baby once again into a sweet slumber, I came out of the bedroom and was walking through, what I thought was the empty living room, when I heard a tiny voice. After investigating, I found the noise to be coming from behind the couch…I tiptoed over and listened.

"And I thought I was her littlest angel," Casey quietly

sobbed.

Oh dear friend, my heart just broke. I realized how badly I had hurt my precious son. I pulled him out from behind the couch and just held him. I explained that my outburst was not his fault, that I was sorry and that I loved him. That incident was one of the biggest wake-up calls in my role as a mom. It was pivotal in making me change the way I communicated with my children.

After the realization, I asked myself two questions.
1. Am I the only one?
2. Is there hope for change?

I was determined to find an answer. I began to interview and survey moms from around the globe on the topic of screaming. Maybe the word scream is too harsh for you. You prefer to use words such as yelling, losing it, flipping out, or whatever sounds more palatable to you. The definition of the word scream is: give a long, loud expressive cry. It really doesn't matter what we call it. We want to change it.

Back to the research. I am a nuts-and-bolts kind of gal, so I was straightforward in my questioning. I cut right to the heart of question.

Do you scream (or yell) and if yes, why?

I want to applaud the honesty of the participants. Of the 300 women, 298 said they had at the very least "raised their voice."

So right away I had the answer to my first question.

I am not alone!

Sigh. What a relief.

After basking in the thought that I had lots of company on the screaming train, I wanted to know: is change possible? For me — as well as the 298 honest moms. I would only find the answer to this if I researched the WHY. Why do we lose it, flip out, yell, or scream? If I have the "why" I could explore the answer to change.

My survey participants had no trouble listing the triggers of why they find themselves flipping out on family members. Either verbally or in written form, story after story tumbled out with an overarching theme of stress, exhaustion, and being overwhelmed with demands.

In studying the various illustrations in the survey results, it became clear that the real culprit in our vocal explosions is not just our children.

Take for example, my vacuum cleaner. My sweeper is a model that requires the user to insert a disposable bag. This bag is intended to be used until full, and then discarded and replaced with a new one. However, I have a habit of ignoring the "full bag" indicator on my sweeper. The bag invariable fills to overflowing, dirt backs up and packs the hose, and finally with no place else to go, debris explodes on my carpet!

The stories shared by the survey participants pointed to this same scenario. Stress, exhaustion, and demands build. Our children may have contributed to build-up to a degree; however, they are often the poor soul who is there when the eruption of words come flowing out. Yes, they play a role, however, in the coming chapters we'll discover the degree in which they contribute to our outbursts.

The *whys* are most certainly there and we'll explore them together. The best news is that there is hope for change. My kids are all grown adults and I wasn't a perfect mom (you'll see in future chapters just how imperfect) but I was determined to stop yelling. It's possible! Stick with me and you will have some new tools and strategies that will help you get off the screaming train.

QUESTIONS:
1. What is your term for screaming?
2. Do your kids respond to the yelling in a negative manner? Hurt feelings, yelling at siblings, etc?

Stress, exhaustion & demands build

Our children are often the *poor soul* who is there when the eruption of words come flowing out.

We can change it.

CHAPTER 3

A View from the Other Side
(How Screaming Affects our Kids)

Some of us may wonder if screaming is really even that big of a deal. "My parents yelled at me and I turned out just fine," is a response I've heard before. I surveyed kids at various ages and these were the responses I got:

> Preschooler: It just makes me sad.

> Grade School: I feel I just can't do anything right.

> Jr. Higher: I get mad and do just the opposite.

> High School: My mom yells at me and I don't know if she realizes her words stay with me for a long time.

Those were the typical responses I got across the board. That alone was enough to make me want to make some major changes, but for our purposes here, I called in a friend and a professional to find out what our habitual yelling does to our kids from a psychological standpoint.

Meet Kathy Koch, Ph.D., author of six books, a speaker, and the founder of Celebrate Kids, Inc.

Here is what she had to say:

When screaming is a mom's habitual response, children don't feel safe. I might go so far as to say they are not safe. Might screaming lead to physical harm? Possibly. Does it lead to emotional and identity harm? What about relationship harm? Absolutely.

Children who are constantly yelled at will not feel secure. They will not be secure. Without security, they'll walk on eggshells around their mom. They won't feel like they have solid footing moving forward, but instead may feel like they're on very shaky ground.

If that was your situation, would you want to be close to the screamer or remain distant? Would you risk trying again to please the screamer or would you give up and decide you're supposed to be screamed at? Would you try to change – to fake it to make it – while resenting the screamer the whole time?

A lack of emotional safety can cause children to give up on themselves and others. All relationships may be unstable because these children will not think well of themselves. If they feel unworthy of support and love, they may present themselves as insecure and timid. This can make it challenging for others to get close. Sometimes children react in opposite ways. Being desperate for someone to accept them, warts and all, can cause them to perform and become perfectionistic to earn love and acceptance. Pride and ego will now get in the way of close relationships with others. The very thing they may be desperate for – a loving, accepting, unconditional relationship – may be impossible. Hope now decreases further.

Of course, for parents to be the habitual screamers is more damaging than if anyone else is. We're supposed to be safe with our parents. We're not supposed to have to question their love for us. They're supposed to be on our side. Moms and dads are supposed to be approachable. They're supposed to be a major source of our peace and security. When they're not, children may question love in general. They may believe they're not worthy of being loved. They may decide it's unimportant. These beliefs can change everything.

If screaming has become a habit, moms may not be able to see improvements children make. This, too, leads to children giving up. Children frequently tell me, "I can't please my mom so I stopped trying. It's easier and it doesn't hurt as much." Now a pattern of low expectations sets in. This "identity harm" is among my greatest concerns. Do children who are habitually screamed at become who God intended them to be? Often they do not. On a rare day when they're not yelled at, they think they were lucky rather than skilled, obedient, patient, good, etc. They reject their abilities and growing character as a fluke. They may never invest in themselves to discover talents and strengths.

Many children tell me they don't want to make their mom mad. Some have asked me if I can help them change. They don't want to be horrible and they do want their mom happy with them. In different ways, they tell me, "Yelling at me doesn't help. I wish she would teach me how to …" They sometimes finish the sentence with a general phrase such as, "be better" and "make her happy." Sometimes they're very specific with endings like, "finish my homework" and "clear the table the way she wants me to." As I say all the time, telling and yelling doesn't help. Teaching does.

How often is our habitual screaming not about our children at all? It's about us — our fatigue, our disappointing day, our impatience, our fear, and more. When this is the case, there's nothing children can do to change our reactions. Yet, they try. They desperately want to be our solution. That's a heavy burden for them to carry. Again, they'll fail. Hope decreases again.

Without hope, life is hard. Children habitually screamed at need it and may never find it.

———

I think we are all aiming to be our children's safe place from the rest of the world. We want to be the person they can count on for love, no matter what. If we are going to build our kids up and give them the confidence they need to go out into the world and face life head on, we have to learn a better way of dealing with our frustrations.

Friends, we can do this. And we must.

We are aiming to be our children's safe place from the rest of the world.

We want to be the person they can count on

no matter what.

CHAPTER 4
Just Another Day in Paradise

"I just keep losing it with the kids. They just don't understand! I am in college full-time, working part-time, and top that off with being a wife and mother. My kids just complain I am not around enough!"

Christy from IL.

Ask yourself, what is at the number one thing that is putting you over the edge?

Seriously, you are having an amazing calm, controlled "indoor mommy voice" day and then, it happens. You lose it. Again.

Do you see a pattern? Tough question. The days I lost it I hardly wanted to document or journal the moment. I would rather just forget it. But stay with me here. People don't just lose it. There is build-up or a trigger. Change begins when we become hyper-aware of our breaking point.

Identifying your triggers is extremely important as we wish to become "scream-LESS" moms. This reality was evident for me years ago. After surviving a stressful morning with three boys under five, I was feeling discouraged, frustrated, and disappointed in my role as mommy. Negative thoughts pierced my confidence as the day dragged on. Mountains of laundry continued to grow in the laundry room and my living room looked as if a category four hurricane had torn through. The boys wanted me to play with them, but I was preoccupied with household tasks and snapped at them to "go play by yourselves." Yeah. It was a tough day.

When the doorbell rang, I answered it clad in an old Aspen tee shirt, shorts, and hair in a ponytail. As I opened the door, the older gentleman on the other side looked at me and asked, "Is your mommy home?" At his inquiry, I burst into tears and exclaimed, "See, even YOU don't think I should be the mommy!" I know he meant well…and it could be taken as a compliment…. however, I just shut the door on the bewildered gentleman.

I slouched down against the closed door and cried, "I really don't want to be the mom today… someone else needs to be the mommy." As the minutes crept by and I continued to lean against the door, I felt this tiny hand on my shoulder and sweet toddler breath on my skin. "I wov you, Mommy," he declared, and laid his head on my shoulder.

Yup, I could do it another day…this motherhood thing. Sometimes encouragement comes in the smallest and most unexpected packages. But what had triggered my outburst?

In examining the morning, it was easy to point out where

the buildup stemmed from. It wasn't my children; it was the laundry and chaotic living room mess. I was exhausted by the mere thought of trying to catch up. Armed with that knowledge, I had hope that change could occur.

Is your blow-up a result of pent-up frustration over the never-ending laundry pile that seems to multiply like rabbits? Just when you are feeling caught up, you find another pile of towels shoved in the corner of your teenager's bedroom. Or maybe it just drives you crazy that your house has not been swept in 3 weeks and then you step on a lucky charm in the living room and as you are pulling the sticky mess from your sock you lose your indoor mommy voice in a major way.

You'll have a sense of empowerment once you can identify what puts you over the edge. Now you can formulate a detour to keep you from reaching the breaking point.

TIPS: If your trigger is the laundry, consider going to the laundromat. Seriously, no eye-rolling please. I did this for a season and it alleviated stress. After dropping my older boys off at school, I headed to the laundromat and as seven machines cleaned and dried the clothes, I read books to my toddler. After folding the clothes, I took them home in baskets and put them away. Seven loads were completely done by late morning. This left the must-have-tonight loads manageable and my indoor mommy voice intact. The added plus for my toddler was reading time with mommy.

One of my triggers was a clean house. I wasn't even aiming for white glove condition. My standards were not that high. I just dreamed of floors and bathrooms cleaned on a semi-regular basis. And furniture dusted often enough that you couldn't write "clean me" in the dust. Armed with this knowledge (revelation of trigger), my husband and I got creative and hired a high school girl to come in every other week after school and help me clean. This stretched an already tight budget and was a luxury; however securing the help of a teenager who was in need of cash was much cheaper than hiring a professional adult.

Now it's time for you to do some homework on yourself. Use the questions and notes below to consider what your triggers might be.

Questions:

1. Commit to noticing (bonus points for making a note on your phone or writing it down) what is

happening around you before you lose it each time in the next week. Identify that trigger and consider yourself Superwoman for now understanding the "what" behind your screaming.

2. Now armed with knowledge, what are some ways to combat those triggers?

You'll have a sense of *empowerment*

when you can identify *what puts you over the edge.*

CHAPTER 5
Not Now, Maybe Later

When my boys were still young, I was offered an amazing opportunity to travel and speak a considerable amount more than I had been. Although it felt wonderful to be wanted, asked and included, my husband and I agreed to pray about it for a few weeks. We both weren't convinced that this was the season in our children's lives for me to take on more responsibility outside the home and be absent more often. The next week, as I was preparing my "speaking stuff" for a different engagement the following day, my youngest son Brock came into the room.

"So, are you speaking tomorrow?" he asked.

"Yes," I replied.

"Where are you going to speak at?" he continued.

"At a church about an hour away," I said absently, as I put the final notebook in my box.

"Are you going to be home when I get home from

school?" he inquired.

"You bet, I will be home several hours before you get here."

"O.K." he said sounding relieved, and left the room.

It was the answer I was searching for. I wanted to throw my arms around Brock, do a little Hallelujah dance and just praise the Lord for giving me His perspective on this opportunity.

"Not now, maybe later."

These words often flow from a mother's mouth when she is answering a request from her kids. Likewise, sometimes moms must adjust to this same response when we are contemplating adding more to our schedule. You see, our children are not interested or impressed that we are on a committee, president of the board, or speaking to women across the country. What they need to know is YOU will be there! Not stressed out, screaming, frustrated, and trying to-do-it-all there… but actually BE THERE! Engaged, warm, loving, relaxed, have-time-for-you there!

Sometimes it's not now, maybe later. Many of you can relate how hard it is to WAIT. There could be financial pressure that makes staying, returning, or working extra hours in the workforce necessary for you. Find ways to cut expenses to decrease the income needed so you don't feel stressed out and frustrated by the workload. My friend Veronica is a single mom and works four ten-hour days a week so she can be home the other three. She swaps after-school care with the neighbor and they carpool the kids whenever possible to save on fuel expenses. She also bought a home near the school so her kids have easy access to before and after-school activities. All of these are little things she did to make sure her kids came first and her stress would be as low as possible.

Questions & Reflection

1. Are you wrestling with an opportunity or a need in your home that will result in being away less? Is this opportunity going to make you a better mom—more present when you are with them and less likely to take frustration on them?

2. If finances are an issue, examine areas of your life you may be able to cut back to relieve some stress. Many stores like Walmart and Target now offer services where you can order what you need and either drive up or walk to a customer service counter to pick up your order. This could be a great time and money saver if you are like me and browse the Target aisles every trip, filling my cart with things I didn't really come in to buy in the first place.

Children are not interested
or impressed if you are
on a committee, president
of the board, or speaking to
women across the country.

———

*They need to know
you will be there!*

CHAPTER 6
The Cost of Saying Yes and the Art of saying NO

Several years ago, I started working at the hospital part-time to help cover skyrocketing insurance premiums. I was often tempted to pick up more hours. I'd tell myself the extra money would be nice to use to upgrade our 8-year-old vehicle, or maybe put in new countertops, flooring, and the list goes on. But, in my heart of hearts I asked myself, was the added income worth the added stress?

Volunteer work needs to be put through the same soul-searching filter.

Is now the time?

An eye-opening and yet heart-wrenching moment in my parenting was when my son asked me why I was so nice to the children I had volunteered to pick up each day on the way to school, but so "mean" to him and his brothers. Yeah, that stung. Yet, he was speaking truth, straight to my heart.

Ask yourself, is now the time to be president of the PTA, chairman of Vacation Bible School, or Girl Scout leader? Should YOU be taking the pot roast, potatoes, carrots, and dessert to your sick neighbor while your children eat spaghettios?

I am not trying to be harsh but maybe someone else can meet the need at this time, and not you. Keep it all in perspective. This is just one season of many in your life.

Giving our best to the people God has given us to take care of and cherish is our number one calling. If you are expending all your best energy on other things, other causes or other people, we're likely going to regret the outcomes of our time investment later down the road. "*What's one more thing going to hurt,*" we console ourselves as we contemplate adding another obligation to our to-do list.

When is the last time you did absolutely nothing for 10 minutes? (Sleeping does not count!) Every moment of your day should not be scheduled. It is unhealthy for you and your children.

An easy way to tell if you are putting your best effort into your husband and children is how they act around you. Does your husband walk on eggshells around you? Have the kids stopped asking you to play or read to them? If your answer is "Yes," you need to assess any new commitment (and probably some of the commitments you already have) before saying yes to anything. Ask yourself these questions first:

> "*Will this benefit my family or me in a positive way?*"

> "*Do I have a passion for this commitment or am I saying*

"Yes"" out of guilt?"

"Is my schedule already full and if so, what will I omit from my schedule to take on a new responsibility?" (No, you cannot omit the kids.)

"Is this an absolutely necessary obligation at this season of my life?"

"What do my husband and kids say about this commitment?" (Your family may have an opinion, if you ask them.)

When I used the above questions to decide whether or not to say yes to a new commitment, making decisions became much easier.

Here's how it looked for us a few years ago. My husband and I decided we wanted to offer the machine shed on our property as a place to "hang out" on Friday nights after home football and basketball games. Understanding that entertaining and feeding up to seventy-five teenagers at our home would be a gigantic commitment, we put some serious thought into it. Using the above questions as a filter our answer was clear.

Would this benefit our family in a positive way?

Absolutely! Not only would our children be at our house, but we would have the opportunity to get to know their friends.

Did we feel a passion for the activity?

Yes, we had the enthusiasm and excitement it takes to

offer the teenagers a safe place.

Would our schedule allow for another commitment?

With planning ahead with food preparation and the entire family's efforts, we were able to add this venture to our calendar with few adjustments.

Is this an obligation for this season of our lives?

We think so; our children are only with us for a short season of time. To invest now in the lives of our children and their friends will have humongous dividends for years to come.

And finally, *what did our children think of this commitment?*

You know the answer to this one!

And so, each night for nearly 9 years, dozens of teens descended on our property, and even though it was a ton of work, it did not put me over-the-edge because I asked the questions before making the commitment.

Questions for your consideration:

1. Do you often say yes out of guilt? If so, have you ever said "no"?

2. So... when is the last time you did absolutely nothing?

Giving our best to the people God has given us to take care of and cherish is *our* #1 *calling*

CHAPTER 7
Overwhelmed

"I told myself I wasn't going to scream today. I had a good morning until I was taking my 8-year-old to school and she announced (when we were almost there) that she had forgotten her lunch. Then her older brother remembered today was "Picture Day," and of course, they weren't dressed for this. I lost it; I screamed all the way home and then lectured them the whole way back to school. I feel like I have "loser" written on my forehead."

Shelley from MO.

Mom, the demands on your time in a single day can be staggering. In one 24-hour-period you can be nurse, chauffeur, cook, housekeeper, laundry matron, counselor, accountant, mentor, coach, lover, and friend. And this list is not exhaustive! Plus, it doesn't include your responsibilities in your full or part-time job.

Someone seems to need us from the minute our feet hit the floor until we fall in bed at night. And often, even in the middle of the night! On call, day or night, we feel we never have a moment's peace.

On one particularly busy day, I hadn't even taken the time to use the restroom. My bladder was screaming for attention and with the boys playing outside, I dashed to the bathroom. I had just sat down on the toilet when Levi, 4, came running into the bathroom. "Mom, hurry up, I need to go right now!" he exclaimed, as he hopped on one foot.

Exasperated, I said "Son, I just sat down, you will have to run upstairs and use that bathroom."

"I can't wait," he said.

"Levi, I am not getting up," I firmly stated. Our dialog continued until Levi, with a look of delight, as if the answer to our dilemma had been discovered blurted, "Mom, you don't have to get up"! "Just scoot up and I will go behind you!"

NO WAY!

Not a moment of peace. Anywhere. Sigh.

Constant demands put us on the fast track to overwhelmed and stressed, which often leads to a ride on the screaming train.

One memory that pops up that I'd like to forget began after hitting the snooze button several times. We were running behind from the very beginning. Seth had a doctor appointment and I awakened the boys with the "everyone move now" voice. You know the one. The one where you haven't quite lost it yet, but you can tell the stage has been set for it to happen. Not long after getting up, our youngest announced he had wet the bed, so sheets were stripped and tossed in the washer.

Meanwhile, I realized our library books were due, along with an overdue DVD. Since we lived 30 minutes from town, we made every effort to make our trips count. As I was rushing the kids through breakfast, I hung the clean sheets on the clothesline outside. While the boys were rounding-up books, they started arguing over who got the front seat. Then an all-out search ensued for the missing DVD, which I found under the couch, along with various petrified food remnants. Just what my mounting tension needed, a cruel reminder of my lack of housekeeping. My frustrations were reaching the boiling point as everyone seemed to be moving in slow motion.

About that time, Brock, my preschooler, knocked his juice off the table and as I was getting a rag from the sink to clean up the mess, I looked out the window and saw our dog, running across the yard, with the sheets in his mouth. I lost it. I screamed. Really screamed.

Looking back now, (isn't hindsight great?) things could have been done differently to alleviate some of the stress. I had set myself up for failure before the day even began.

What would it have looked like if I had set myself up for success instead?
1. Get the entire family up 15 minutes earlier than needed every day. This leaves room for emergencies, because they will happen.

2. The night before, all family members lay out clothes for the next day. You too, mom.

3. Determine the night before all appointments/ errands you will make the following day and prepare for them. Bank deposits, library books, grocery list, sporting equipment and clothing, permission slips, etc., are all gathered and ready.

4. Have your children put all shoes, coats, lunch bags, and backpacks by the back door.

5. Teach your older children how to do laundry and have them start an emergency load in the morning, if needed.

6. Resist the urge to add "anything" to your morning schedule unless you planned for it.

7. Have a chart for who gets to sit where and when in the car if this is a source of frustration for your family. A plan takes the argument out of the equation.

These are just a few "tweaks" I made in our morning routine which made a colossal difference in my day and set me up for success instead of failure. It sounds like a lot to do the night before, but if we are taking care of things for the next day, we'll have space each day to take care of the non-planned things (dog + sheets) without those fun surprises sending us over the edge.

Questions

1. Do you agree that being overwhelmed is the last straw in a series of emotions that shuts you down?

2. Do you find one (or several) situations that consistently make you feel overwhelmed?

CONSTANT DEMANDS
put us on the fast track to

overwhelmed

& stressed

which often leads to a
ride on the screaming train.

CHAPTER 8
Communication is the Key to Success

"I am pulled so many ways, with my aging mother, and kids still in the home, I feel like my head is going to pop off. When frustrations build up over the care of my mother, I scream at the kids, even though it is not their problem."

Lisa from OH.

Open communication, especially during times of change, can be a great way to keep off the bumpy road of being overwhelmed and stressed, which often leads to losing it with our kids. Explaining to our children about the extenuating circumstances such as aging parents, financial hardship and illness can keep you from becoming a pressure cooker about to blow. Like a pressure cooker, you only have a window of time to remove the pan from heat before it will explode. You definitely want to watch the pot very carefully. Taking time to discuss with your children a reason (age appropriate) as to why you may be on edge, can help everyone be more sensitive to the circumstances.

Your family will be far more willing to pitch in and help make the situation easier if they know a few details as to why mom is touchy.

Kids appreciate open communication, and they usually have no trouble telling it exactly like they see it. I was exercising on the floor in the living room and Brock was lounging on the couch working on his laptop. I should share with you that on a scale from 1-10 in the area of athleticism, I am a negative four. I am pathetic. I cannot even run to my mailbox and back without falling. It's true, but that's another story. Anyhow, I was trying to work out to this new exercise DVD. Ten minutes into the exercise routine Brock looked over at me lying on the floor in a shape resembling a pretzel.

"Mom, are you supposed to look like the lady in the video?" he asked.

"Yes!" I said enthusiastically, quite pleased that he had noticed my skill.

"Well, you don't."

Yeah, like I said, children appreciate an honest, transparent answer similar to the responses they sometimes give to us. The candid communication style may help us as moms keep our cool when the heat is turned up. This open communication style with our teens can keep a conversation from turning explosive. No one wants to engage in a heated exchange we will later regret.

Our son Levi made some very unwise choices in his late teen years that tested his dad and my patience to the limit. Quite often tempers and voices would rise in frustration at another destructive choice made.

One of those despairing times was a midnight call from Levi. Still groggy with sleep I remember bits of the brief explanation that included words such as, police, underage drinking, water tower and the plea "*Will you come pick me up?*".

It wasn't hard to find him in a small town; I just followed the flashing lights that illuminated the sky.

After I had a brief conversation with the police officer, Levi got in the passenger seat and we began the drive home. Immediately, he began his side of the story. I stopped him. "*Son, I am upset and disappointed and I do not want to discuss this. Not one more word. I am sure you have a lot to tell me and we will talk in the morning when our emotions cool down.*"

There was no shame in leaving the battlefield that night. I knew I was one breath from an explosive reply. Open communication with our son (telling him we were not going to talk about it at that time) simply de-escalated the situation and it was able to be handled the next morning without the conversation turning nasty.

After the conclusion of a parenting conference, a mom walked up with a pained look on her face. "*Sue, my home is a combat zone and I scream daily.*"

I asked her to share with me the number one thing that is putting her over the edge. *"My daughter's room; It is a pigsty and we argue about it daily"*, She explained.

I suggested she try an experiment. *"Close the door to your daughter's room. Communicate to her that the door is to remain closed at all times. If she needs laundry done, she is to do it herself."*

A week later I got an email from the mom. *"We have had the best week in months. I have not yelled once. My daughter and I actually had some very sweet conversations."* Yes, in a perfect world the daughter would be compliant and cleaned her room. And not all moms could handle the known mess behind the door. However, we are exploring what puts moms over the edge. This mom was wise to recognize a conversation with her teen needed to take place, explaining she was purposely hitting the pause button (by closing the door) and letting the tension rescind. Hopefully, her daughter would get sick of living in squalor in the near future. In the meantime, get her an extra tetanus shot.

We need to keep in the forefront of our mind that we are raising the next generation of spouses, employers, co-worker, neighbors, parents, and friends. We all appreciate when we are given an honest explanation to the emotional overload someone may be carrying. It creates a deeper sense of empathy for the person and the awareness may encourage us to help lighten their load or at the very least stay out of their way.

TIP: Share with your child when you feel like you are at the tipping point. For preschoolers, simple words such as, "Mommy is sad and her sad is turning mad so I am going to put myself in timeout for 10 minutes" (and set a timer).

For older children it may be more specific such as, "Grandma fell and broke her hip today. She is at the hospital resting. This is very stressful time for me. I need extra help for the next few days until we can move her to a comfortable rehab facility. Can I count on your help in this area _____?" Be specific.

Questions for you

1. Are you specific (age appropriate) about the circumstances (behavior, illness, finances) when you communicate to your family that may affect your mood?

2. What's one benefit you could see from being more communicative about your feelings with your kids?

THERE IS NO SHAME IN
LEAVING THE BATTLEFIELD.
it creates space for the
situation to *de-escalate.*

CHAPTER 9
If I Could Just Get a Full Night's Sleep!

Every day was the same. I would wake up exhausted and the first thing on my mind was, "I wonder if I can get a nap in today?" I trudged through many days, in a fog, counting the hours until bedtime. My exhaustion affected my mood which bled over into EVERYTHING. My overall negative attitude made my triggers easily tripped. By 7:30 a.m., my indoor mommy voice was nowhere to be found.

Mothers are tired.

According to Health@NBC News (November 10, 2015) of 500 mothers interviewed, 54% claim they are not sleeping enough.

. Of the mothers working full-time, 50% state they sleep 6 or fewer hours a night.

And 48% of the stay-at-home moms stated they are sleep-deficient.

The survey confirms that no matter what working status is,

moms are not getting enough rest. They live in a world of seemingly never-ending fatigue.

Lack of sleep is serious business. Loss of sleep leads to dramatic dysfunction in blood sugar levels, metabolism, mood, memory, and immunity. Emotional stability is particularly affected.

Sleep deprivation makes you spend your days in a literal daze, feeling forgetful, and out of sorts. Emotions can go haywire leading to an inability to judge situations appropriately. Even with our best intentions, we feel helpless and overreact. Poor sleep cripples us and we have very little chance at maintaining an indoor mommy voice.

When you and I close our eyes at night, our brain and body work together to renew and rejuvenate our bodies.

Even one night's worth of poor sleep affects your performance the next day and if that cycle continues, research published in the Journal of the American Medical Association, says you are 15-20% likely to be clinically depressed.

Missing several hours of sleep just one night causes you to feel angrier, sadder, more stressed, and more mentally exhausted than normal. Night after night of poor sleep can push you beyond your limits.

I remember as a young mom an elderly woman in church told me I needed a hobby. I looked at her and questioned, "How about sleep? Is that a hobby? All I want is sleep."

Adequate sleep seemed elusive, always just beyond my grasp. I longed for uninterrupted sleep. I would even daydream of a full night of sleep. As the sleep deprived nights progressed, my emotional outlook became poorer. Short-fused and ill-tempered was the norm as I began each day.

This fatigue and emotional weariness did not go unnoticed by my husband and we started to investigate creative ways that would enhance the quantity and quality of my sleep.

When we had an infant in the home, I started to go to bed as soon as the evening feeding was complete. This meant sacrificing time with my husband in the evening; however, a temporary forfeit until our babies' sleep patterns elongated. My husband would then stay up and feed the next feeding with a bottle. By going to bed at around 8 p.m. (soon after the preschoolers were tucked in), and my husband taking the 11 p.m. feeding shift, I would have approximately 6 hours of sleep before the 2 a.m. hunger cries began. We continued this "team approach" for several weeks and this plan made a tremendous impact on the sleep deprivation I was experiencing. I woke up in the morning with a clearer mind and better attitude to start my day.

Even as our children grew older we used the team approach. This protected each of us from bearing the weight and negative effects of interrupted sleep. I took naps whenever the children napped, which was very hard to do when faced with mountains of laundry and dishes. However, leaving dishes undone or floors unswept by going to bed early or squeezing in a nap is a small price to pay for an emotionally stable mommy who can keep her cool with the kiddos.

Tag team sleep (even for a few weeks) can make a huge difference. Sometimes our team sleep approach didn't go quite as planned. I remember the night, after falling into blissful slumber, being brought back to consciousness by one of my children crying in his bedroom. Stumbling into my son's room I had discovered he had lost his pacifier, again. Levi had 5 pacifiers, and upon dropping, they liked to congregate under his crib. Why five? Since birth, Levi was a light sleeper. And even now at 21 months old, he often awoke during the night and simply wanted the comfort of his pacifier to fall back to sleep. My type-A husband, Curt, grew tired of fumbling around in the dark each night trying to retrieve a fallen pacifier, bought five of them and lined them up on the dresser. Curt and I took turns each night responding to Levi's cries and having multiple pacifiers, guided by the glow of the nightlight, created a seamless (we could do it half sleeping) routine. Half sleeping, I reached for the next pacifier only to discover all 5 were under his bed.

Pregnant with our next child, I got down on my hands and knees and tried to "fish" around for one of the pacifiers. Not feeling any of them, I scooted, my eight-month pregnant body, further under, to continue my search. Upon doing so, my back hit the lever under the side of the crib that lowers it, and the side came down "trapping" me underneath. All that was sticking out were my legs. At this point, my toddler was screaming, and I was helpless, although somewhat victorious, in finding all five lost objects, called out for my husband, above the screams. You can imagine his surprise, when he entered the room, turned on the light, and found only my legs sticking out from under the crib. He was a wise man, not to ask, "What are you doing under there?" I certainly wasn't dusting.

Moms need to be protective of their quality of sleep even when their children are older. When our boys reached an age where we didn't have to listen for a "cry in the night" we invested in a "sound machine" for our bedroom. One of the best investments we have ever made. Whether it was the heavy footstep of an older child retrieving a glass of water or the noise of a teen watching a weekend late night movie, the white noise from the sound machine masked the disruptive sounds so we could sleep without interruption.

Being intentional is the key to healthy, restorative sleep. Incorporate the following suggestions and see if your fatigue level decreases.

1. Set a schedule: If possible, get up and go to bed about the same time each day. Your body becomes habituated to falling asleep at a set time.

2. Go dark: Make your bedroom as dark as possible. The darker the better. Light interferes with the production of melatonin. Purchase blackout curtains If needed. And adjust the LED light on your alarm clock to emit the least amount of light.

3. Turn off electronics: Start your nighttime electronic fast thirty minutes before bed. Studies show the lights from electronics are melatonin-suppressive and can affect sleep. And if you charge your phone near your bed, flip it upside down so any alerts you get won't light up the room.

4. Exercise: A poll conducted by the National Sleep Foundation found that exercisers rarely have sleep problems. This can be as simple as a 20-minute brisk walk on the treadmill or a run in the park. Any exercise will help promote sleep.

5. No evening alcohol: Yes, you may fall asleep quickly but it will disrupt your later sleep cycles. If you enjoy a glass of wine, drink it early, four to six hours before you go to bed, so it will not interfere with your sleep.

6. No caffeine after 2 p.m.. It can take six to eight hours to eliminate caffeine from the system. Some people are more sensitive to caffeine than others. Refraining from your afternoon pick-me-up can increase quality of sleep.

7. Turn the heat down. You will sleep better in a cool room than one too warm. A cool room helps lower your body's core temperature, aiding in sleep.

Implementing a few creative changes helped me get the rest I needed to be a mom who used her inside voice. Most of the time.

Questions for you:

1. From the tips above, which one(s) can you implement tonight to get better sleep?
2. Is lack of sleep a factor for you in the battle against yelling?

Missing several
hours of sleep a night
causes you to feel
sadder, more stressed
and more
mentally exhausted
than normal.

CHAPTER 10
Find Your "Hiding Place"

My toddler threw a tantrum in the grocery store, my preschooler was defiant, and my preteen was disrespectful. All before 10 a.m. My indoor mommy voice was long gone.

I wanted to run away. Far away.

Becoming more conscious of my triggers, I learned to identify a need in my life. A hiding place.

When? Where? How?

Hear me out. You will continue to hit your trigger and flip over the edge if you don't intentionally pursue a hiding place.

A refuge of respite.

It need not be costly nor complicated. For years my most frequented hiding place was the walk-in closet in our master bedroom. Several times a day I would slip into this unlikely sanctuary and take a moment. To sweeten up my hiding place, I even kept a one pound bag of M&M's hidden up on the shelf. I would count out 15 (I still don't know why 15) and sit on the floor and eat them.

Alone.

Glorious.

I didn't need a sitter and I knew exactly where my children were. They were banging on the bedroom door. "Mommy, whatcha doing?" It was simple, yet so very effective when I felt ready to lose control. A break just for me. A moment for the triggers to settle or diffuse.

Hiding places, creative spaces. Just for you.

My friend Cristy loves scrapbooking. She told me how it relaxes her and she totally unwinds when creating beautiful memories for her family. Convinced I would enjoy it too, she invited me to a "crop til you drop party." I arrived, purchased over $100 in scrapbooking supplies, and "cropped" until I became frustrated; which took all of 30 minutes. Clearly, this was not my answer to respite.

Sweet co-worker Amy finds her reprieve in exercise and invited me to join her at Zumba. As mentioned before, my athletic ability on a scale from one to ten is a -4. I am not an athlete. I embrace this fact. At my resistance to join her, Amy explained that anybody can do this exercise. I must not be "anybody" because I looked and felt like an idiot. So I crossed exercise off my hiding place quest.

My neighbor Cindy is a single mom. She works full-time

outside the home in addition to raising two active boys. She parents alone and there is no one at home to take over for even an hour to give her respite. I asked her how she carves out a hiding place. Cindy explained that three days a week she picks up the boys a half hour later from daycare. During that half hour, she goes to a nearby park, sits on a bench and reads. Even in the cooler months she will sit in her car in the park reading. Just her, in her hiding place.

There are times you may need a longer stretch of respite. When our sons were teenagers, I desperately needed a break. Tensions were high and I certainly wasn't using my patient mom voice. I shared my need with my husband, hoping he could join me. After some discussion, we reasoned the finances were not available for a get-away and our children were not mature enough to be left alone overnight. But my wise husband encouraged me to go. He suggested I go to a nearby hotel and spend the night. Alone.

He didn't have to tell me twice. That Friday I threw my bag in the car, hugged my four sons and man, and drove to the nearby hotel. On the way there I went through the drive-through of my favorite restaurant and took it with me. And there I was, in that king-size bed, with my favorite food, watching a chick flick and deliriously happy. What triggers? The next day I checked out and went home with myself fully intact. I had respite. A hiding place.

Your hiding place may look very different than mine or your best friends'. It must recharge YOU. Maybe Zumba, yoga, or running is your hiding place. It may be crafts or a good book. Walking through a bookstore with a good cup of coffee is a hiding place for some moms. Or maybe a coffee shop visit alone every Saturday morning is your hiding place. Whatever it is, make it a priority. Arrange a sitter or talk to your husband about watching the children or running carpool so you can have your anticipated time of respite. Often. You will be amazed how it diffuses the trigger that causes moms to flip out.

More hiding place ideas to explore:

Gardening, Bible Art Journaling, Nature Walk, Hallmark Movie marathon, knitting, massage, puzzles...

Maybe your most treasured hiding place will be turning off your cell phone for one hour. Now that's respite!

Questions:

1. Do you have a hiding place? Is it giving you the respite you need or do you need to change it up?
2. If you don't have a hiding place, what are some ideas of creating one? Make a plan, try it for two weeks and see if it exactly what you needed.

Your hiding place
may look very different
from your best friends.

It must recharge
YOU.

CHAPTER 11
Master rather than Victim

I waited in the driveway of the babysitter's home. She usually came bounding out when I came to pick her up. The boys were growing restless in the hot van, so after a few moments I got out and walked to the door. When our sitter, Amy, answered the door, she had a confused look on her face. "Oh, Mrs. Heimer, I must have forgotten you needed me today. I will be ready in a moment."

After dropping the sitter and the boys back at the house, I rushed to my hair cut appointment. I was frustrated that the sitter was not ready and now I was late. I partially ran through the door of the salon and spotted another client already in the chair. "Oh, no." I thought to myself. She already gave my appointment away.

However, upon seeing me enter the shop, my sweet hairdresser had a bewildered look of confusion. I had seen that look earlier: on my sitters face.

"I am so very sorry I am late" I explained.

"You're not late", she stated. "You don't have an appointment today. It is same time, same day, NEXT week."

I went home and apologized to the babysitter.

That night I was discouraged and overwhelmed. Through tears of frustration I shared my blunder with my husband. "I am 'spinning' so many plates I can't keep them straight."

My husband is a wise man. He knows when I just want to be listened to and when I need a plan of action. I was looking for an answer to my disorganized life.

I remember stating, "I want to be the Master of my day and not the victim."

Curt, is a type A, organized and disciplined by nature. I am not. He lovingly asked where the "day planner" was that he had given me a few weeks before. I retrieved it and he looked at the day. "Sue, all you have on today's calendar is 'Take Seth to preschool.' We both know you did far more than this today. Why are they not all listed in your planner?"

He was right. I overscheduled myself on a regular basis. Being frustrated with myself and not wanting to repeat the rut I was stuck in, I started to write down EVERYTHING in my day planner. Soccer practice, preschool, church youth group, dry cleaners, even tasks like laundry and dishes. It gave me a clearer picture of my day. This also gave me freedom to incorporate the word "no" when asked to add something to my day, often using the full calendar as my excuse. When I started writing everything down, I wasn't surprised that I had been overwhelmed. I should have been. I was packing way too much in my day. And my triggers were being hit like a pinball machine.

In just a few days, my head felt clearer and I felt a welcomed sense of control. The victim feeling started being replaced with Master. A master with an indoor mommy voice.

> **TIP:** Each one of us know how much we can have on our schedule before reaching our tipping point. We all have limits. What's yours? Do you need two afternoons each week with nothing on the calendar? Or maybe three evenings with no planned activities? Whatever you need, keep it sacred. Right now, go through your calendar and mark off the margin you need each week to keep sane. So your child won't be able to participate in karate, hockey, debate club, piano and be on the competitive swim team, but, he will be a more balanced child because his momma isn't nuts.
>
> I take this concept even farther with my personal planner. I look ahead at my calendar and I ask myself, "Is there any white space left? Wiggle room?" Even if my sacred spots are reserved, I evaluate the week in its entirety. If I sense that commitments in the upcoming weeks are putting me into the danger zone of overcommitment, stress, exhaustion, etc., I put a yellow highlighted line right through the days of the week. That

indicates WEEK CLOSED. Nothing is added to that week. NOTHING. No last-minute appointments, birthday parties or play-dates. This simple line through my calendar has been one of the most freeing tools as a mom. When the week is closed, it is closed. I am the master of my days and not the victim!

Your calendar may be on your smartphone, tablet or traditional paper. Whatever works for you is perfect. Put everything on it including family time and margin for those unforeseen trips to the doctor.

Questions for you

1. Have you ever missed an appointment or showed up somewhere at the wrong time? Describe how you felt when you realized your blunder.

2. Do you have a true sense of everything that is on your daily schedule? If you have a planner, *FILL IT OUT!* If not, buy one, download one, or create one for yourself.

Become the

master

of your day & not
THE VICTIM.

CHAPTER 12
Will You Be My Hero Baby

"Some days I do really well. I am patient and calm. Then comes bedtime, and I blow it. I feel guilty ending the day yelling at my kids in frustration."

Mary from AZ

It had been a long day. By 6 p.m., I was exhausted. My husband was in the living room unwinding with the sports channel and I was trying to wrap up my day with a few household chores.

As I lugged the overflowing laundry basket through the living room with a toddler dragging on my leg, my husband turned his attention toward me and asked, "Do you need any help?"

Of course, I did. However, I like many women, think, *"Good grief, if he can't see I need help, I am certainly not going to tell him."*

I promptly responded, "No. I am fine."

With a shrug of his shoulders he turned his attention back toward the television.

In just a few moments he could tell it was the wrong question and response. (It could have been my passive-aggressive stomping through the house). What happened next is engraved on my heart forever. Curt met me in the laundry room where I was folding yet another load of laundry, looked me in the eyes and said, "I want to be your hero. I want to be 'that guy' who rescues you. But, you have got to let me. When you say you are 'fine' I assume you are fine. When you say you don't need help, I will take your word that you don't need my help. I am a guy — I do not see your needs. You need to tell me what you need from me so I can be your hero."

That evening I shared with him the number one thing he could help with that puts me over the edge. Even on a good day.

Bedtime routine.

By 7:30 p.m., I am toast. I have been on mom duty for over 13 hours. My brain is fried and my patience spent.

So that very night he suggested I go take a warm bubble bath and he would take over the bedtime routine. He didn't have to ask me twice.

The next morning, as I prepared breakfast, the boys, still clad in their pajamas came bounding down the steps into to kitchen. The first thing I noticed is that each one of them had their p.j.s on backwards.

As a woman, the first thing that came to mind was to point out to my husband his error. Thankfully, I had a check in my spirit that said, "Thank him again for putting the boys to bed and say nothing about the mistake."

I knew from experience that if I criticized Curt's sincere efforts it would have hampered any future attempts. He would have thought, "*Why even bother to help. I cannot do anything right. I will never measure up to her standards.*" By having a heart of gratitude and thanking him, he felt like the hero that he was and had quality time with our sons each evening. Plus, it took just a few days and the pajamas were worn correctly without my intervention.

Questions

1. Are you holding back from asking for help because you are scared, too proud, super particular about the ways things are done, or because you feel guilty? Identify why you don't ask for help (taking the responsibility on yourself) and then write out some things you can ask for help from your spouse, your kids, your mom, or another support person in your life.

2. Do you thank the people in your life when they do something kind for you to help? Showing gratitude usually encourages the giver to give more freely the next time.

ASK FOR HELP

from your spouse,
your kids, your mom,
or any other support
person in your life.

CHAPTER 13
Consistency and Your New Best Friend

'I wake up and say, 'today I will be consistent' and that lasts until 7:30 a.m."

Juanita from Texas

I am convinced that the only way to maintain an inside mommy voice is to become consistent. I have a love/hate relationship with the word. A consistent mom is what I call "Velvet over Steel." She says what she means and means what she says. Always. It is the *always* part that gets me.

Does this sound familiar?

1. You walk into a room riddled with toys and declare, "I want this room picked up in ten minutes!" Then you go back to doing whatever you were doing before said declaration and forget you even gave an instruction.

2. Your children do not respond to your instruction using your "indoor mommy voice". They wait until your frustration rises to the point where you

yell, "Pick up your toys!" Then they think; "*Now she means it.*"

3. Bedtime or morning routines are only accomplished through repeated instruction, threats, bribes, or screaming.

If any of these are a regular occurrence in your home, buy a kitchen timer. Please buy three of them because your children will hide them.

My consistency as a mother skyrocketed with this small but mighty purchase. If you wonder if your child is too young or too old to introduce a timer, I encourage you with these parameters.

Depending on the maturity of your toddler, I would introduce the "timer" at 24 months of age.
If your teen is still struggling with the above tasks they are not too mature to introduce the timer.

How implementing use of a timer works:

1. First, establish clear expectations and clear consequences. Children want clarity. It makes them feel secure. For older children, you may want to make a list of expectations and consequences and post it in your home.

2. Introduce the timer to small children by showing them how it works. For instance, "Alex, I am going to set the timer and we have ten minutes to pick up the living room toys. If the toys are not picked up by the time the timer goes off, we will have to stand in the corner for five minutes and then try again."

Walk them through it and purposely not finish the task, so they get the idea of the consequences. When your time in the corner is finished, set the timer again to ten minutes and this time finish the task before timer sounds. Do this at least 3 days in a row so they know the expectations.

3. Older children can be instructed verbally. Be clear on your expectations (i.e. living room straightened in 5 minutes) and the consequences (no video games for evening). Set timer and let them respond if they want to complete the task or pay the consequences.

4. This works beautifully with bedtime routine. For instance, you explain to your children that you are setting the timer each night and they have 20 minutes to get ready for bed. This would include showers, teeth brushed, clothes laid out for next day, book bags by back door, pajamas on, and waiting in bed for prayers. Keep it age appropriate. Even four year olds can have teeth brushed and pajamas on and waiting in bed for a bedtime story.

The expectation: these tasks are accomplished and they are waiting in bed for you to come say goodnight when the timer sounds. The consequences: they must go to bed fifteen minutes earlier the next night and you continue to move the time up until they have successfully completed bedtime routine and are in bed in the allotted time. No yelling or losing it. It is their choice whether they want to beat the timer or pay the consequences.

5. The timer is also effective for morning routine as well. The same concept as nighttime. I would wake the children (older ones set their own alarm) and set the timer. They had twenty minutes to make bed, brush teeth, get dressed, etc. This kept them on task without my saying a word. No shouts of "hurry up or we will be late."

When the timer sounded, they needed to be in the kitchen for breakfast. Consequences for not being in the kitchen when timer sounded was an extra chore after school for older children (ex. Sweep entire upstairs, clean bathroom, dust) and no after school snack for younger children.

*The consequences you choose may be different than the ones we incorporated. Only you know the natural bent of your child and what would be an appropriate punishment for not meeting basic expectations.

We used the timer for everything and adjusted it as our family grew and developed. Get creative. If the timer can help you keep your indoor mommy voice, then use it. Often.

Questions for you:

1. How can you incorporate the timer into your routine?
2. What will be the consequences if a task is not completed when timer sounds?

Establish clear expectations & clear consequences.

CHAPTER 14
Expectations vs Consequences

The concept of "Expectations versus Consequences" will follow your child into adulthood. You are doing your children a favor by introducing it at a young age. Remember, you are raising someone else's future spouse, employee, employer, neighbor, and friend. As long as they breathe, there will be expectations by others and consequences if they do not meet them.

There are consequences if:

an adult does not show up for work.

if you "forget" to pay your employees.

if you do not mow your yard and the grass grows 2 feet tall.

if you do not stay faithful to your commitment to your spouse.

when you are always late for a lunch date with a friend.

All of the above are just a few examples of the expectations that your child will encounter as an adult.

Now equate that to losing it with your child. What if you have trained them to only respond or meet expectations when you yell? When the volume of your voice gets above indoor mommy voice?

What will happen if they only meet expectations under these circumstances? Will they not show up to work until the boss calls and screams on the phone? Or when the neighbor becomes unglued with the length of the grass? Or their friend finally "blows up" when they are habitually late?

When we continue to use the volume of our voice as the means of motivation, we are potentially setting our children up for failure as an adult. We are giving them an unrealistic view of an adult world.

Consequences from lack of follow-through or completion of a task will be part of their lives forever. You are doing your child a favor by incorporating realistic expectations and natural consequences into their lives at a young age.

When choosing expectations, always keep in mind your children's ages, however they usually can do more than you give them credit for.

A four-year-old should be able to scrub a toilet and a two-year-old can gather the trash bags from bathrooms. They can also set the table (if you are concerned about dishes breaking, switch to paper plates for a season.) Put the dishes within reach of the preschooler so they can set the table unaided.

Feeding the dog, emptying the dishwasher, folding clothes and putting them away, dusting, sweeping, wiping counters are just a few ideas, depending on the child's age, that can be incorporated as expectations. These chores are not difficult to learn or teach and can ease your trigger of being overwhelmed. This starts to shift responsibility to your children. Adding more difficult tasks as they mature is a progression that will serve them well when they graduate and move to college or on to the workforce. Delegating responsibility to your children is a vital part of parenting.

Questions

1. Have you set up the expectation of yelling as the only time you are serious about something?
2. Are you getting your children involved in activities that will teach them expectation and consequences? How can you incorporate those this week?

When we continue to use
THE VOLUME OF OUR VOICE
as the means of *motivation*,

we are potentially
setting our kids up for
failures as adults.

CHAPTER 15
Consequences and incentives

A common source of contention in many homes is uncompleted chores. When you are already feeling the strain of being stressed and then discover that the tasks you delegated are not completed puts many of us over the edge. The yelling stems from the frustration that you finally were willing to ask for help. Bring in the troops. Get your kids to step up and take on some of the chores that do not require an adult to accomplish them; and they let you down. They didn't come through as you hoped. Discouragement leads to raised voices.

I had worked at the hospital all day and came home exhausted with a carload of groceries. As I got out of the vehicle, I noticed our dog standing by the dog dish with a look that told me she had not been fed today. Exasperated, I made a mental note to ask Casey why his chore of feeding the dog hadn't been done. After pouring some food in her bowl and adding fresh water to her pan, I stumbled through the door with a load on my arm eager to get them put away and relax for a few minutes before starting supper. Upon entering the kitchen I discovered that there were dirty dishes cluttering the counter. Putting the bags on the floor, I felt frustrated. Seth was in charge of dishes that day and obviously they were not done. My plan of having a few moments of respite vanished as I knew that by the time dishes were completed, the supper and homework routine would need to be in full swing; and the groceries still not put away. My expectations (the dishes done and the dog feed) had not been met and I felt instantly overwhelmed. I yelled — loudly.

Obviously, some changes needed to be made to give incentive for tasks to be completed. These incidents showed that the consequences for not getting them accomplished were not motivation enough. We needed to up the ante on the penalty for not meeting expectations.

My husband and I had a family meeting that night at the chore chart that hung in the kitchen. He reinforced that all chores needed to be completed by 4:30 every day. No exceptions. When the clock struck 4:30 any chore not completed would be offered for "sale" to another sibling. Each chore would cost $3 to be paid to the sibling that completed it for you. If no sibling was interested in doing your chore for $3 then mom or dad would do it. However, a parent's time is very valuable and the cost is double or $6 if they complete it. Let me assure you. Children hate paying a sibling from their allowance.

It did not take too many missed chores for the boys to start completing their assigned tasks by 4:30 p.m. And there always seemed to be a sibling waiting by the chore chart at that time to see if they could make any extra money. Tasks started being completed and my stress trigger received some reprieve.

Remember, your children are capable of more than you think they are. Expect them to contribute to the operation of your family home. Everyone has a part and it builds teamwork within the family unit.

Question for you:

1. You manage a home, not a hotel. What chores could you assign to your children to relieve some stress?

YOUR
CHILDREN
ARE CAPABLE
OF MORE
THAN YOU
THINK
THEY ARE.

CHAPTER 16
Cutting the Attitude

What stressed me when my children were little changed as they got older. I thought I was done with the screaming years. Boy, was I wrong.

Leslie from CA

When pinpointing my stress triggers as a mom of tweens and teens I would admit that my two top tension builders were my child's attitude and name calling.

Your child's attitude can greatly affect your stress level which increases your chance of losing it with your little miss-know-it-all. We all have moments. But when those moments morph into longer periods, everyone is affected.

Name calling is very destructive on the person being attacked. Your home should be a safe place for *all* of your children. It is their haven and hiding place from the world. Name calling has no place in this or any environment.

To curtail these to stressors in our home we implemented

a pay-the-jar system.

I put four jars in the cupboard shelf, representing each of our sons. Then one extra jar on behalf of the family jar. Each week, I would line up four stacks of ten one dollar bills (each child had 10 ones) next to their respective jars. Any money left in their stack at the end of the week was theirs to keep.

If they had a bad attitude, I would set the timer and tell them they had 5 minutes to get over their attitude (this included a chance to talk about what was causing the behavior also). When the timer went off, they had to pay the "family jar" a dollar for each minute that passed (beyond the initial five) that they continued to display a bad outlook. This puts the decision back on the child. They must determine, "Is my attitude worth the money (sacrifice) that I will have to pay?" This is a life lesson that they will take into adulthood.

The pay the jar system also worked for banned words and name calling. Calling another child a name or cutting them down with verbal words cost them three dollars in the sibling's jar that they offended. And using inappropriate language in general cost each child three dollars per word in the family jar.

This jar method was instrumental in holding our sons accountable to acceptable behavior and attitude. It took the pressure off of me. There was no screaming, yelling, or lectures; we simply walked over to the jar cupboard and moved the money into the appropriate jars.

This stress-busting idea can be tweaked, depending on the age of your children. Quarters instead of dollars may be more incentive for younger children and older teens may need to be enticed with higher stakes.

If you have a very rebellious child, they may get discouraged by losing all the money in their stack each week. If this is the case, I encourage you to flip the concept and have them earn money when they change their attitude in the allotted time or go without calling another sibling names for a set time period. It may take a few weeks of trial and error to find out how it is best utilized in your family.

Question for you:

1. The Attitude Jar can be altered to fit the greatest stressor in your family. In what way would the Jar system best support you and your family as this time?

Your home should be a

safe place

for all of your children.

It is their

haven

from the world.

CHAPTER 17
Perfect Imperfection

My ah-ha moment when I found my Casey behind the couch (back in Chapter 2) confused and heartbroken changed the course of my communication style with my children. Realizing the damage my yelling was creating and becoming hyper-aware of triggers that led me to lose it was the catalyst for change.

Five years ago, our Casey married his high school sweetheart. The long-anticipated day of the wedding arrived and I was a nervous wreck about the mother-son dance. Did I tell you I can't dance? Nope, it's hopeless. I even hired a dance instructor before the wedding and after a frustrating 2-hour lesson he candidly suggested I stick with the junior high shuffle.

After the beautiful ceremony and toasts were completed, my 6 foot 4, handsome, third-born son led me to the dance floor. As we started to shuffle in a circle, I started a teary-eyed dialog, "Casey, I am so sorry I wasn't always the mom you needed...." Before I could continue, he interrupted me, looked right into my eyes and said "Mom, you were the best mom a boy could hope for."

No sweeter words had ever been spoken. In Casey's eyes, I was the best mom. All the times I had blown it and erupted like a volcano, when I should have stayed in control, I was still "best." And you, dear reader, are the best mom for your child. You are the imperfect best mom. Let that sink in.

Road trips with our van full of boys was always a wild ride. You never knew what surprise or emergency would be part of the journey. However, one predictable conversation always ensued. "Mom, are we there yet? How much longer?" And I would respond, "not there yet... but, we are getting closer!" Ten minutes later the same conversation would start all over again. "Mom, are we there yet?"

Mom, you may not be "there" yet. You may not be the scream-free mom you want to be. But, you are getting closer. Closer to the confident controlled mom who asks and accepts help, establishes expectations with appropriate consequences, says what she means and means what she says, builds respite into her life (M&Ms count), learns to say no and forgives herself. Keep starting new each morning, lean into your friends or spouse to keep you accountable, and forgive yourself while asking your kids for forgiveness when you mess up.

You are the most perfect imperfect mom for your kids.

YOU

are the imperfect

best mom.

Endorsements

"With compassion and honesty Sue gives practical hope and help for the frazzled, frustrated and feeling "on the edge" mom. Her questions to ponder will help you pull up the roots of those frustrations and failures and plant seeds to help love, joy, peace and tender care grow in your heart.

Pam Farrel, international speaker, author of 45 books including *7 Simple Skills for Every Woman: Success in Keeping It All Together*

"With hope, humor, and practical ways to change, Sue Heimer helps the frustrated mom trade in screaming for something much better. Your family will like the difference and so will you."

Arlene Pellicane, speaker and author of *Parents Rising: 8 Strategies for Raising Kids Who Love God, Respect Authority, and Value What's Right*

This is the friend to friend guide I wish I would have had when my kids were little (and beyond...). I love that it is packed with tips that real moms can start implementing today, for better relationship tomorrow and beyond.

Kathi Lipp, Best Selling author of *The Husband Project Clutter Free and Overwhelmed*

I am around moms on a daily basis. I consistently see frazzled moms on the edge because of little self-care, busyness, and overwhelmed by life today. Sue Heimer offers very practical tools to help Moms not lose their cool and thrive in their relationships with their children.

Jennine Ulibarri, Director of MOPS, La Casa de Cristo Lutheran Church

"I can't believe I said that. I'm sorry, sweetheart. Please forgive me." I wasn't exactly "winning" at motherhood the day I realized I was habitually saying unkind things to my kids—things *that I didn't even mean*. Blame it on stress, call it bad parenting... the net result was the same—I was wounding my precious kids and I wanted to do better. If you can relate, here's hope: author Sue Heimer gets right to the core of why we yell. Without sending moms on another guilt-trip, Sue identifies common struggles and directs readers to the ultimate source of wisdom and healing: God's Word. Every mom needs this book!

Heidi St. John, Speaker, Author of *Becoming MomStrong*, Founder of MomStrong International

Moms, this book will be your lifeline. I have deeply appreciated Sue's insight and wisdom for a long time – and have been begging her to write this book for years! All of us, as moms, know we have things that set us off, and we often feel helpless to break the cycle. *Practical Help for Frustrated Moms* is the solution. In these pages, you'll find a road map to identifying your triggers and exactly how to change them. Even better, you'll be encouraged on the journey. I know you'll enjoy your time with Sue as much as I do!

Shaunti Feldhahn, social researcher and best-selling author of *For Women Only* and *For Parents Only*

As a licensed psychologist and professional coach, I see too many moms struggle with their emotions and wait until a crisis before they are willing to say I need help. Sue Heimer's personal experiences will show you that you are not alone. In *When you feel like Screaming* she offers real hope and practical strategies to dramatically improve your well-being and that of your family. This is a much-needed book to equip and empower any frustrated, frazzled mother who just wants to scream.

Georgia Shaffer, professional certified coach, PA licensed psychologist, and author of *Taking Out Your Emotional Trash and A Gift of Mourning Glories*

Through Sue's authenticity, wisdom and real life examples, she affirms that you are not the only one who loses it, and there is indeed, hope for change. Sue offers practical advice that works, so you really can set yourself up for success and your kids will believe you are the best Mom in the whole world.

Lisa Rose, Founder of The Gatehouse and Project HandUp

Have you ever screamed at your kids? If so, you're among friends. Most moms have experienced moments when the mommy monster shows up. We don't like it, we don't want it to happen, we don't know what to do about it. This book, however, gives you the way out. Sue Heimer has been there and she has wisdom for all of us to savor. Goodbye mommy monster...the future looks bright without you hanging out in my home.

Jill Savage, author No More Perfect Moms

Do you feel frustrated and frazzled on your motherhood journey? Thankfully, in her book, *When you Feel like Screaming: Practical Help for Frustrated Moms,* Sue is a trusted friend who walks with you on the journey to find your "indoor mommy voice." She offers hands-on, effective solutions versus more mommy shame. Get this book, friend. You—and your family—will be happy you did.

Cindy Bultema, Executive Director of GEMS Girls' Clubs, speaker, Bible teacher, and author of *Red Hot Faith* and *Live Full, Walk Free: Set Apart in a Sin-Soaked World*

LET'S STAY CONNECTED

Now that we're friends, let's stay connected. One of the best ways is by signing up to receive my free quarterly newsletter for encouraging and helpful resources.

So sign up at www.sueheimer.com and let's stay in touch.

You can also find me at www.facebook.com/sueheimer

Better yet, invite me to speak at your next women's event. I love encouraging and equipping women in all ages and stages of life. One of my greatest joys is meeting women face-to-face at conferences, retreats and events. Contact me at www.sueheimer.com to inquire about my joining you at your next event!

Made in the USA
Lexington, KY
01 May 2018